T0071053

Circlesong

Bob Chilcott

for upper voices, SATB, and piano
or 2 pianos and percussion

vocal score

MUSIC DEPARTMENT

OXFORD
UNIVERSITY PRESS

OXFORD
UNIVERSITY PRESS

Great Clarendon Street, Oxford OX2 6DP,
United Kingdom

Oxford University Press is a department of the University of Oxford.
It furthers the University's objective of excellence in research, scholarship,
and education by publishing worldwide. Oxford is a registered trade mark of
Oxford University Press in the UK and in certain other countries

© Oxford University Press 2020

Bob Chilcott has asserted his right under the Copyright, Designs
and Patents Act, 1988, to be identified as the Composer of this Work

First published 2020

All rights reserved. No part of this publication may be reproduced,
stored in a retrieval system, or transmitted, in any form or by any means,
without the prior permission in writing of Oxford University Press

Permission to perform this work in public (except in the course of divine worship)
should normally be obtained from a local performing right licensing organization,
unless the owner or the occupier of the premises being used already holds a licence
from such an organization. Likewise, permission to make and exploit a recording of this work
should be obtained from a local mechanical copyright licensing organization

Enquiries concerning reproduction outside the scope of the above
should be directed to the Music Rights Department, Oxford University Press,
at music.permissions.uk@oup.com or at the address above

ISBN 978-0-19-354043-9

Music and text origination by Katie Johnston

Printed in Great Britain on acid-free paper by
Halstan & Co. Ltd, Amersham, Bucks.

Contents

Scoring iv
Instrumentation iv
Composer's note v
Texts vi

INTRODUCTION

1. Beauty before me/We wait in the darkness (tutti choirs) 2

PART 1: BIRTH

2. Song for Bringing a Child into the World (tutti choirs) 12
3. Newborn (SATB choir) 26

PART 2: CHILDHOOD

4. Yaqui Song (upper voices) 28
5. A Child's Song (upper-voice solo) 31
6. Give me strength (tutti choirs) 32

PART 3: LOVER

7. Chinook Songs (tutti choirs) 39
8. Over the Wave (SATB choir) 45

PART 4: ADULTHOOD

9. Summer Song (tutti choirs) 50

PART 5: MIDDLE AGE

10. O Great Spirit (SATB choir) 59

PART 6: OLD AGE

11. In the house made of dawn (tutti choirs) 68

PART 7: DEATH

12. Farewell, my brother (upper-voice solo) 82
13. The sun's beams are running out/We wait in the darkness (tutti choirs) 84

Scoring

This revised version of *Circlesong* is scored for upper voices and SATB.

A separate part for upper voices is also available (ISBN 978-0-19-354372-0).

Instrumentation

The accompaniment to this work exists in two versions:

For small ensemble

2 pianos and percussion (4 players):

1. marimba
2. tubular bells, triangle, wood blocks
3. tam-tam, bongos
4. timpani, hi-hat, tom-toms

Full scores, vocal scores, and instrumental parts are available on hire/rental from the publisher's Hire Library or appropriate agent. For small ensemble performances, the piano parts available on hire/rental should be used, rather than the part in the vocal score.

For one piano

The pianist plays from the vocal score.

Composer's note

I have found in my work, in my past as a singer and latterly as a composer, that an overwhelming sense of discovery, curiosity, inspiration, knowledge, and the desire to understand the rich tapestry of the human condition, has opened up to me through words that I have either sung or set. As someone who grew up singing the Christian liturgy on a daily basis, I have found great solace in setting Biblical texts, hymns, and psalms. I have also read and set a great deal of secular poetry in English and for a number of years have worked in collaboration with living poets. The text and the words become the vehicle for whatever musical discourse and picture I wish to present.

In the late 1990s I became very interested in indigenous poetry after reading a book of prayers (in English translation) from many different cultures. I set a number of these prayers and poems and, soon after, was inspired to write a larger work, a life-cycle piece based on translated poetry of indigenous tribes of North America; the text to *Circlesong* is drawn from the Chinook, Comanche, Dakota, Inuit, Iroquois, Kwakwaka'wakw, Navajo, Ojibwa, Pueblo, Seminole, Sioux, and Yaqui traditions. A recurring image in the poetry was that of a circle and I became fascinated by this. On a musical level the circle is the shape of the musical notehead, a written symbol that comes to life through sound. The circle is the shape of our world, of the sun, and of the moon. The circle symbolizes day and night, the pattern of the seasons, and the cyclical roundness of our natural world. The circle also symbolizes our interdependence and, most importantly, our unity as a human family. I found a beautiful poem, 'Song for Bringing a Child into the World,' written on the page in the shape of a circle and this set me on my way. I decided to cast this piece within a concept loosely modelled on the seven ages of man—Birth, Childhood, Lover, Adulthood, Middle Age, Old Age, Death—using these beautiful poems ultimately to articulate the importance of living life with care and respect, not only for our world but also for ourselves and each other, with all that that entails.

Circlesong was written in 2003 for the Birmingham Festival Choral Society and City of Birmingham Young Voices, and premiered in Birmingham, UK, in 2004. The work was revised in 2019 for Robert Simpson and the Houston Chamber Choir and the Treble Choir of Houston, and this version was first performed in Houston in February 2020. It is scored for upper-voice choir, mixed choir, two pianos, and four percussion players.

Duration: *c.*40 minutes

This note may be reproduced as required for programme notes.

Circlesong *was jointly funded by Arts Council West Midlands and the Birmingham Local Education Authority. It was first performed by BFCS and CBYV on 3 April 2004 in the Adrian Boult Hall, Birmingham, conducted by David Lawrence and Jeremy Patterson.*

Texts

1. Beauty before me/We wait in the darkness

Navajo/Iroquois

Beauty before me,
Beauty behind me.
Beauty, beauty.

We wait in the darkness!
Now no star is glowing;
Now no sun is shining;
Help in our journey.

Beauty below me,
Beauty above me.
Beauty, beauty.

2. Song for Bringing a Child into the World

Seminole

Let the child be born
circling around you day sun
you wrinkled skin circling around
circling around you daylight
you flecked with gray circling around
circling around you night sun
you wrinkled age circling around
circling around you poor body

3. Newborn

Pueblo

Newborn, on the naked sand
Nakedly lay it
Next to the earth mother,
That it may know her;
Having good thoughts of her, the food giver.

Newborn, we tenderly
In our arms take it,
Making good thoughts.

Housegod, be entreated,
That it may grow from childhood to adulthood,
Happy, contented;
Beautifully walking
The trail to old age.

Having good thoughts of the earth its mother,
That she may give it the fruits of her being.
Newborn, on the naked sand
Nakedly lay it.

4. Yaqui Song

Yaqui

Many pretty flowers, red, blue, and yellow.
We say to the folk, 'Let us go and walk among the flowers.'
The wind comes and sways the flowers.
They all are like that when they dance.

Some are wide open, large flowers, and some are tiny little flowers.
The birds love the sunshine and the starlight.
The flowers smell sweet.
They all are sweeter than the flowers.

5. A Child's Song

Kwakwaka'wakw

When I am grown up
I shall go and stoop digging clams.
When I am grown up
I shall go and splash in the water digging clams.
When I am grown up
I shall stoop down digging clams.
When I am grown up
I shall go picking berries.

6. Give me strength

Sioux

Give me the strength to walk the soft earth.
Give me the eyes to see and the strength to understand
that I might be like you.
With your power only can I face the winds,
All over the earth we are all alike.

Look upon these faces of children without number
and with children in their arms.
With your power only can I face the winds
and walk the good road to the day of quiet.
Give me strength.

7. Chinook Songs

Chinook

Aya!

I don't care if you desert me,
Many other folk are in the town.
Soon I'll take another one,
That is not hard for me!

Whose sweetheart has gone away?
My sweetheart has gone away!
You do not like me!
I know you.

Very unhappy I was in Victoria.
Nobody said good-day to us in Victoria.

8. Over the Wave

Ojibwa

Who, my friend, makes this river flow?
The Spirit—he makes its ripples glow.
But I've a charm that can make the tide
Bring you over the wave to your lover's side.

Who, my friend, makes this river flow?
The Spirit—he makes its ripples glow.
Yet every blush that my love would hide,
Is mirror'd for me in the tell-tale tide.

And though you sleep on the farthest isle,
Round which these dimpling waters smile.
Yet I've a charm that can make the tide
Bring you over the wave to your lover's side.

9. Summer Song

Inuit

Aya! Aya! Ayaya.
It is beautiful when the summer comes at last.
Aya! Aya! Ayaya.
It is beautiful when the reindeer begin to come.
Aya! Aya! Ayaya.
When the roaring river rushes from the hills in summer.
Aya! Aya! Ayaya.

10. O Great Spirit

Dakota

O Great Spirit, whose voice speaks in the wind,
whose breath gives life to all the world.
Hear me!

I am small and weak, I need your power and wisdom,
Let me walk in beauty, let my eyes be glad
beholding the red and golden dawn.

Make my hands touch all things you have made with love,
Make me wise that I may understand the sacred teachings you have taught.
Help me, help me learn the lessons hidden in every leaf and every stone.

Help me, help me.
I seek strength not to be greater than my brother
but to conquer the enemy within myself.

Make me ready to come to you always with a pure heart and with clear eyes,
so when my life fades away, like the setting sun,
my spirit may come to you with honour and without shame.

O Great Spirit, whose voice speaks in the wind,
whose breath gives life to all the world,
Hear me! Hear me! Hear me!

11. In the house made of dawn

Navajo

In the house made of dawn,
In the story made of dawn,
On the trail of dawn,
O talking God!

Your feet, my feet restore,
Your limbs, my limbs restore,
Your body, my body restore,
Your mind, my mind restore,
Your voice, my voice restore,
Your plumes, my plumes restore.

With beauty before you,
With beauty before me,
With beauty behind you,
With beauty behind me,
With beauty above you,
With beauty above me,
With beauty below you,
With beauty below me,
With beauty around you,
With beauty around me.

In the house of evening light,
From the story made of evening light,
On the trail of evening light,
It is finished in beauty.

12. Farewell, my brother

Navajo

Farewell, my brother,
When the showers pass over you,
And the thunder sounds.
And when the harvests ripen, and you hear voices
Of all the beautiful birds,
You will say, 'There is the trail of his soul.'

13. The sun's beams are running out/We wait in the darkness

Comanche/Iroquois

The sun's beams are running out.
The sun's yellow beams are running out.
The sun's beams are running out.

We wait in the darkness!
Now no star is glowing;
Now no sun is shining;
Come show us the pathway;
Help in our journey.

We shall live again,
We shall live again,
live again, again.

Circlesong

to City of Birmingham Young Voices with David Lawrence
and Birmingham Festival Choral Society with Jeremy Patterson
who commissioned and premiered this work

CIRCLESONG

BOB CHILCOT

INTRODUCTION

1. Beauty before me / We wait in the darkness

Navajo / Iroquois

© Oxford University Press 2004 and 2020

Printed in Great Brita

OXFORD UNIVERSITY PRESS, MUSIC DEPARTMENT, GREAT CLARENDON STREET, OXFORD OX2 6DP
The Moral Rights of the Composer have been asserted. Photocopying this copyright material is ILLEGAL.

5
oo
Beau - ty be - hind me.
11
mm
mm
poco rit.
A little quicker ♩ = c.66
Beau - ty, beau - ty.
poco rit.
A little quicker ♩ = c.66

15
UPPER VOICES
T./B.
TENORS & BASSES unis.
mp
We wait, we wait in the
p dolce
19
T./B.
dark - ness!
We wait, we wait
22
cresc.
in the dark - ness, dark - ness!
cresc.
25
mf espress.
Now no star is glow - ing;
Now no sun is
mf

28
f
T.
B.
shin - ing,
shin - ing,
f
31
unis. p
shin - ing;
p
35
mp
We wait in the dark -
S.&A. unis. mp
We wait, we wait in the dark - ness!
mp
We wait, we wait in the dark - - -
mp
We wait in the dark - - ness, the
mp

38
- ness!
We wait
We wait, we wait in the
- ness!
We wait, we wait in the
dark - ness!
We wait in the
41
cresc.
in the dark - ness, dark - ness!
div.
mf
No
cresc.
dark - ness, dark - ness!
S.
A.
mf espress.
Now no star is
cresc.
dark - - - ness!
mf espress.
Now no star is
cresc.
dark - ness, the dark - ness!
mf espress.
Now no star is
cresc.
mf

44
ER
CES
star;
No
sun
is
S.
A.
glow - ing;
Now no sun is shin - ing,
T.
B.
47
f
shin - ing,
shin - ing;
f
shin - ing,
shin - ing;
ff
Come show us the
f
ff
f
ff

50
ff
Show us the way; Our jour -
path - way; Help in our jour - ney.
53
mf
mp
- ney. No star,
mf
mp
Now no star is glow - ing; Now no sun is
mf
mp
mf dim.
mp

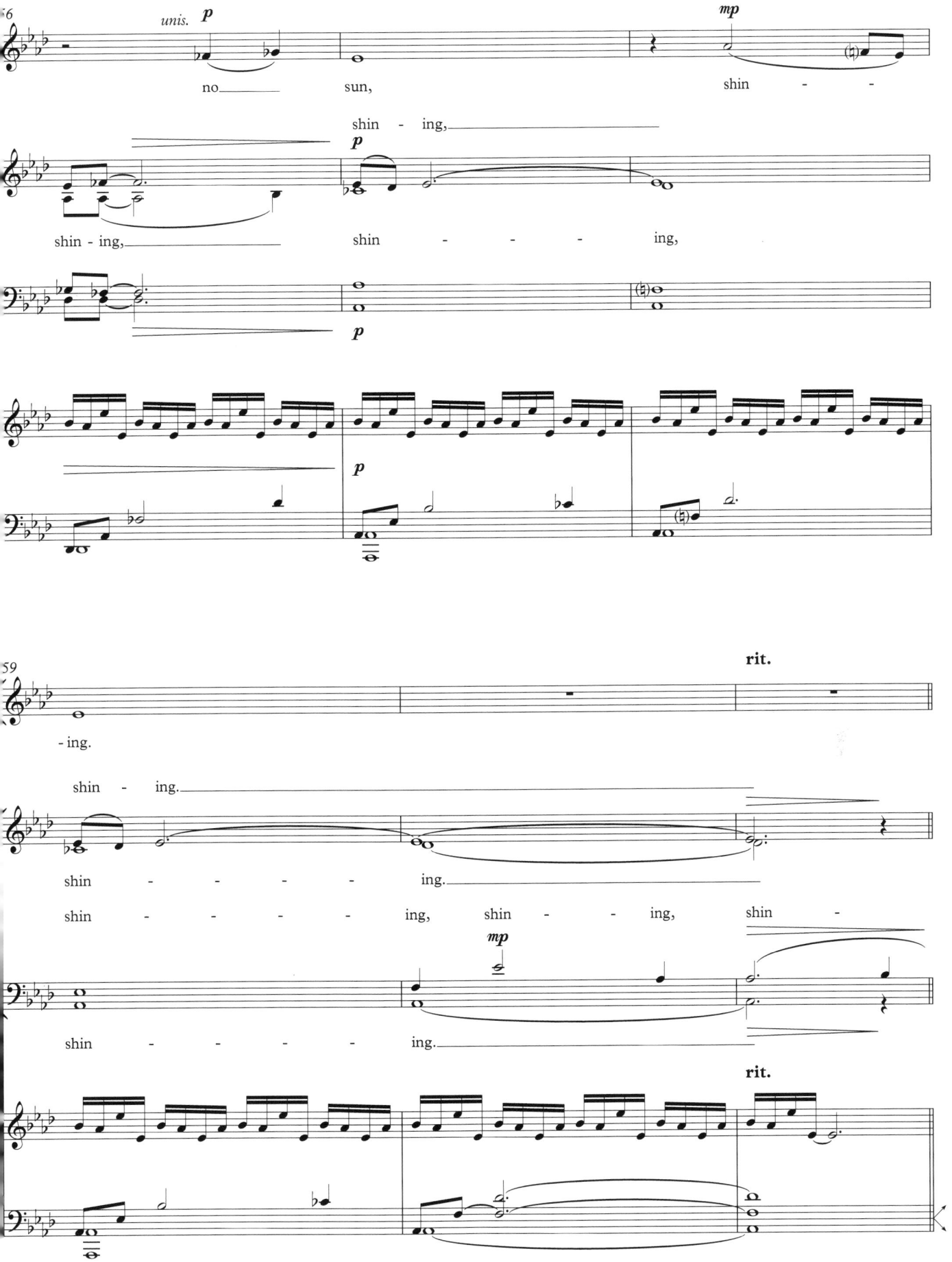
56
unis.
p
no
sun,
mp
shin - -
shin - ing,
p
shin - ing,
shin - - - ing,
p
p
59
rit.
- ing.
shin - ing.
shin - - - - ing.
shin - - - - ing, shin - - ing, shin -
mp
shin - - - - ing.
rit.

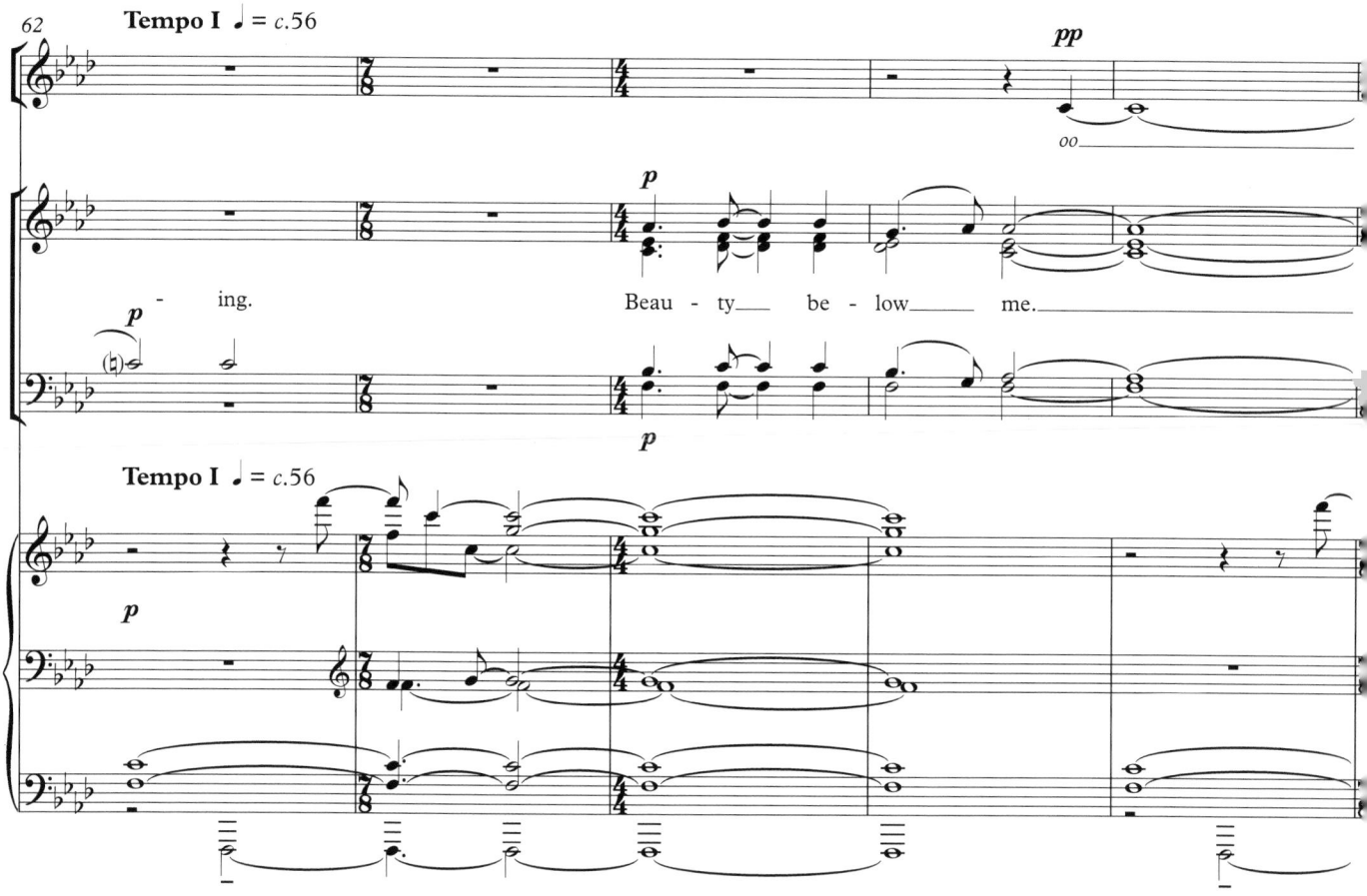
62
Tempo I ♩ = c.56
pp
oo
p
- ing.
Beau - ty be - low me.
p
p
Tempo I ♩ = c.56
p

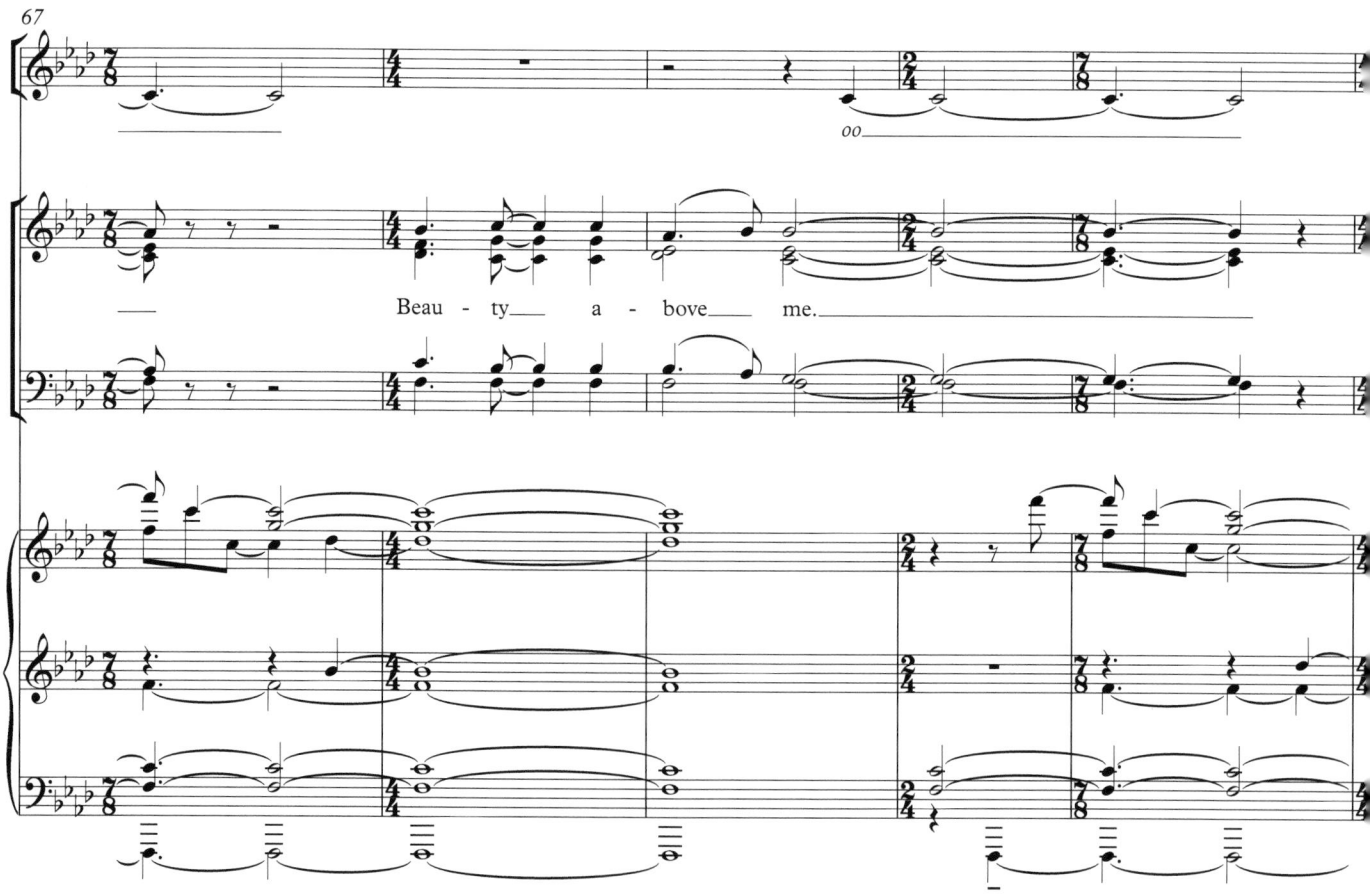
67
oo
Beau - ty a - bove me.

72
p
mm
mm
mm
p
Beau - ty,
beau - ty,
beau - ty,
p
p
77
pp
mm
mm
pp
beau - ty,
beau - ty.
pp
pp

PART 1: BIRTH

2. Song for Bringing a Child into the World

Seminole

ALTOS
p
Cir-cling a - round.
SOPRANOS
p
Cir-cling a - round.
Cir-cling a - round.
Let the child be born,
mp
mp
let the child be born,
Cir-cling a - round.
Cir-cling a - round.
S. let the child be born,
A. Cir-cling a - round.
mp
Cir-cling a - round.
mp

* pronounced 'eye-ya'

06
A - ya, a - - - - ya, a - - ya.
S./A. unis.
mf
Cir - cling, cir - cling, cir - - cling,
Cir - cling, cir - cling, cir-cling a - round.
109
cir-cling a - round.
A.
Cir-cling a - round.
T.
B.
Cir-cling a - round.

112
A - ya, a - ya,
S.
You day sun, you wrin - kled skin.
B.
Cir-cling a - round.
Cir-cling a - round.
115
a - - ya, a - ya.
Cir-cling a - round.
You day sun, you wrin - kled skin.
Cir-cling a - round.

18
a - ya, a - ya, a - ya.
f
A - ya, a -
Cir-cling a - round.
f
unis.
Cir - cling,
Cir-cling a - round.
f
unis.
Cir - cling,
poco f
121
- ya, a - ya, a - - ya.
cir - cling, cir - - cling, cir-cling a - round.
cir - cling, cir-cling a - round.

124
A - ya, a - - ya, a - ya, a - ya.
Cir - cling, cir - ling, cir - - cling,
Cir - cling, cir - cling, cir-cling a - round.
127
cir-cling a - round.
ff
S.
A.
You day - light, you flecked with gray.
T.
B.
ff
f

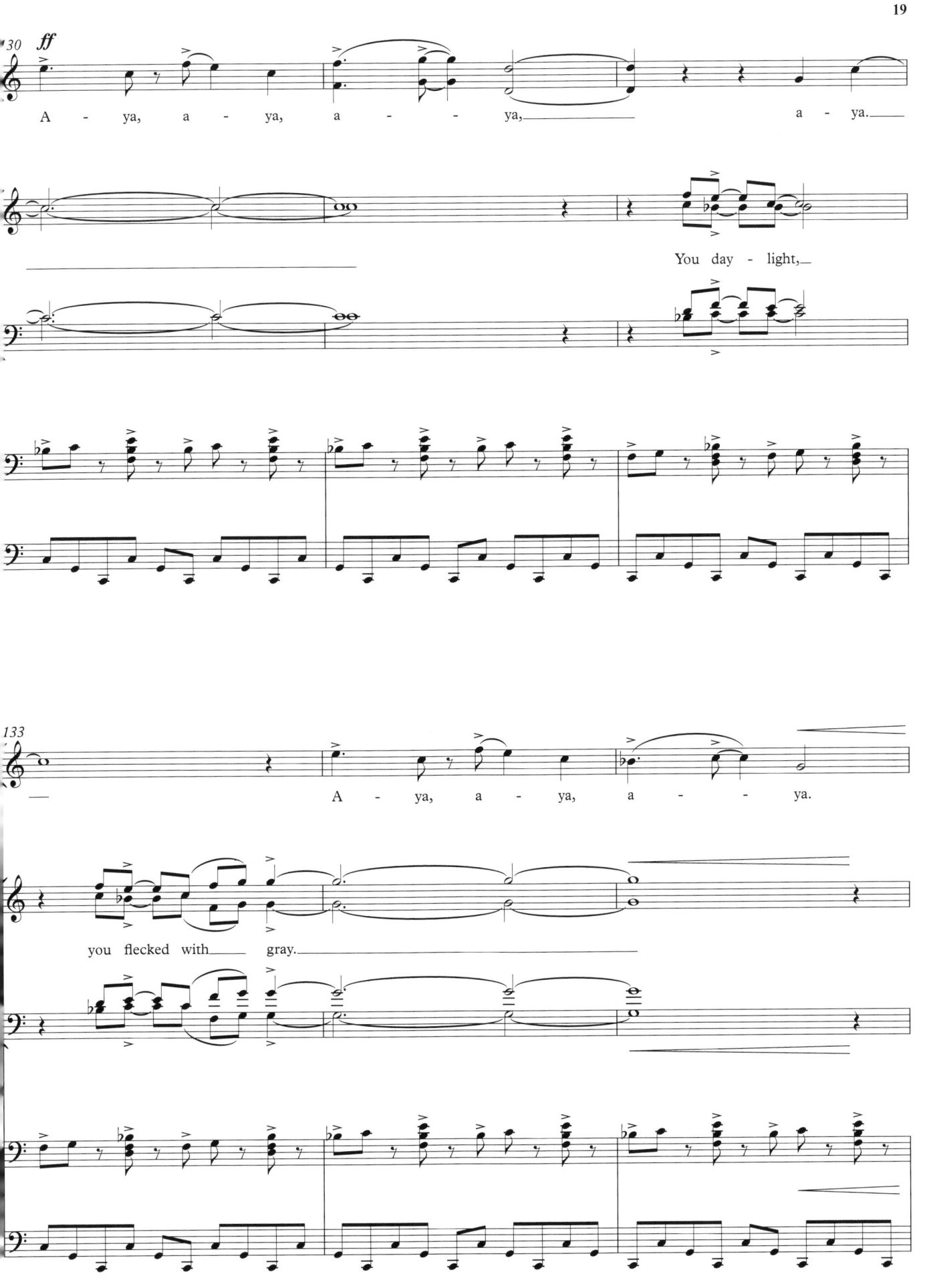
30
ff
A - ya, a - ya, a - - ya, a - ya.
You day - light,
133
A - ya, a - ya, a - - ya.
you flecked with gray.

136
sub. f dim.
A - ya, a - - ya, a - ya, a - - ya.
unis.
sub. f dim.
Cir - cling, cir - cling, cir - - cling,
unis.
sub. f dim.
Cir - cling, cir - cling, cir-cling a - round.
sub. f dim.
139
mf dim.
Cir - cling, cir - cling,
mf dim.
cir-cling a - round.
Cir - cling, cir - cling,
mf dim.
Cir - cling, cir - cling,
mf dim.

42
cir - cling, cir - cling.
cir - - cling, cir-cling a - round.
cir-cling a - round.
mp
Cir-cling a - round.
mp
145
mp
Cir-cling a - round.
ALTOS
Cir-cling a - round.
T.
B.
Cir-cling a - round.

148
Cir-cling a - round,
p
Cir-cling a - round,
cir-cling a - round,
mp
You night sun,
you wrin - kled
age.
mp
p

151
cir-cling a - round.
You night sun,
you wrin - kled

54 Cir-cling a - round,
cir-cling a - round,
Cir-cling a - round,
age.
157
PER CES
cir-cling a - round,
cir-cling a - round,
cir-cling a - round.
160
pp
PER CES
p
S. A.
You poor bo - dy.
T. B.
p
pp
p

164
UPPER VOICES
Cir-cling a - round,
p
p
Cir-cling a - round,
167
UPPER VOICES
cir-cling a - round,
cir-cling a - round,
cir-cling a - round,
S. A.
SOPRANOS & ALTOS unis. mp
Let the child be born,
T. B.
170
cir-cling a - round,
cir-cling a - round,
cir-cling a - round,
let the child be born,
unis. mp
Let the child be born,
let the child be born,

73
cir-cling a - round,
pp
pp
cir-cling a - round,
cir-cling a - round,
p
let the child be born,
let the child be born.
p
let the child be born,
pp
176
cir-cling a - round.
let the child be born.

3. *Newborn*

Pueblo

99
mf
cresc.
House - god, be en - treat - ed,
That it may grow from child-hood to
mf
House - god, be en - treat - ed,
cresc.
206
f
a - dult - hood,
Hap - py, con - tent - ed;
Beau - ti - fully walk - ing
The
f
Hav - ing good thoughts of the earth its mo - ther,
211
mp
mm
trail to old age.
Hav - ing good thoughts of the earth its mo - ther,
mp
mp
mm
mm
217
That she may give it the fruits of her be - ing.
221
pp dolce
rit.
New - born, on the na - ked sand
Na - ked - ly lay it.
pp dolce

PART 2: CHILDHOOD

4. *Yaqui Song*

Yaqui

233
They all are like that when they dance.
236 unis. f
dim.
mf espress.
Some are wide o - pen, large flowers, and some are ti - ny lit - tle flowers. The
f
dim.
239
birds love the sun-shine and the star - light. The flowers smell sweet.
mf espress.

242
S.
They all are sweet-er than the flowers.
f
Ma-ny pret-ty flowers,
A.
They all are sweet-er than the flowers.
f
Ma-ny pret-ty
f

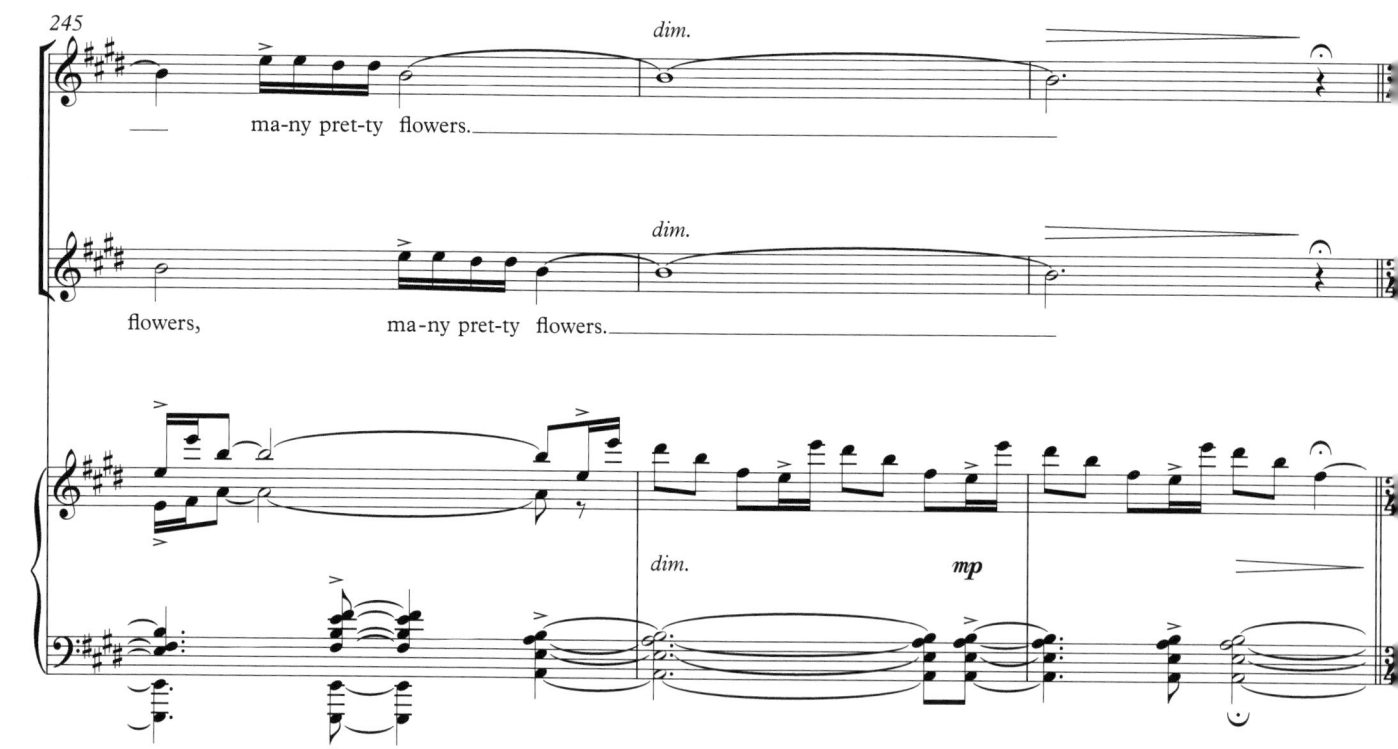
245
ma-ny pret-ty flowers.
dim.
flowers,
ma-ny pret-ty flowers.
dim.
dim.
mp

5. A Child's Song

Kwakwaka'wakw

6. *Give me strength*

Sioux

79
pp
Give me the strength to walk the soft earth.
p
Give me the strength to walk the soft earth. Give
pp
282
Give me the eyes to see
cresc.
and the strength, the
me the eyes to see
cresc.
and the strength to un - der -
cresc.
285
strength to be like you.
mf
f
With your power on - ly can I face the
- stand that I might be like you.
mf
f
f

288
winds, All o - ver the earth we are all a - like. With your
291
UPPER VOICES
f
With your power can I face the winds.
S. A.
power on - ly can I face the winds, All o - ver the earth
T. B.
unis.
294
S. A.
p
we are all a - like.
(p)
Look u -
T. B.
p
(p)
p

297
-pon these fa - ces of child - ren with - out
300
num - ber and with child - ren in their
303
ER
CES
p
Look u - pon, u -
S.
A.
pp
arms.
Look u - pon these
T./B.
pp
pp

306
-pon these fa - ces of chil - dren with - out num-ber
fa - ces of chil - dren with - out num - ber
cresc.
309
cresc.
and with chil - dren in their arms. With your
mf
cresc.
and with chil - dren in their arms. With your
mf
cresc.
mf

12
f
power on - ly can I face the winds and walk the good road to the
f
power on - ly can I face the winds and walk the good road to the
T.
B.
f
f
315
day of quiet. With your power can I face the winds.
day of quiet. With your power on - ly can I face the winds and
unis.

318
S.
A.
walk the good road
to the day of quiet.
p
T.
B.
p
p
321
poco rit.
poco rit.
324
a little slower
rit.
pp
UPPER VOICES
Give
me
strength.
pp
S.
A.
Give
me
strength.
T.
B.
pp
a little slower
rit.
pp

PART 3: LOVER

7. Chinook Songs

* pronounced 'eye-ya'

338
cresc.
in the town. Soon I'll take a - no - ther one, That is not hard for
cresc.
342
mf A - ya! A - ya! A - ya! A -
mf A - ya! A - ya! A - ya!
f
me!
f
mf
346
- ya! A - ya!
A - ya!
ALTOS mf
Whose sweet - heart has gone a - way? My sweet - heart has

50
cresc.
f
gone a - way! You do not like me! I
cresc.
A - ya! A - ya! A - ya! A -
354
mf
mf A - ya! A - ya! A - ya!
know you.
f
mf
358
- ya! A - ya!
A - ya!
TENORS & BASSES unis.
mf
Ve - ry un - hap - py I was in Vic -

362
cresc.
-to - ria. No - bo - dy said good - day to us in Vic -
cresc.
366
mf A - ya! A - ya! A - ya! A -
mf A - ya! A - ya! A - ya!
f
-to - ria.
f
mf
370
UPPER VOICES
- ya! A - ya!
A - ya!
S.
f
I don't care if you de - sert me, Ma-ny o-ther folk are
A.
f
Whose sweet - heart has gone a - way? My sweet - heart has
T./B.
(unis.) (f)
Ve - ry un - hap - py I was in Vic -
f

374
cresc.
in the town. Soon I'll take a - no - ther one, That is not hard for
gone a - way! You do not like me! I
ff
- to - ria. No - bo - dy said good - day to us in Vic -
378
SOPRANOS ff
A - ya! A - ya!
ALTOS ff
A - ya! A - ya! A - ya! A - ya! A - ya! A -
ff
me! I don't care if you de - sert me, Ma-ny o-ther folk are
know you. Whose sweet - heart has gone a - way? My sweet - heart has
- to - ria. Ve - ry un - hap - py I was in Vic -

382
A - ya! A - ya!
- ya! A - ya! A - ya! A - ya! A - ya!
in the town. Soon I'll take a - no - ther one, That
gone a - way! You do not like me!
- to - ria. No - bo - dy said good - day to
385
A - ya! A - ya!
A - ya! A - ya!
is not hard for me! A - ya!
I know you. A - ya!
us in Vic - to - ria. A - ya!

8. Over the Wave

Ojibwa

400
rit.
rit.
cresc.
f dim.
a tempo
404
mf espress.
poco cres
Who, my friend, makes this ri - ver flow? The Spi - rit — he makes its rip - ples glow. Yet
mf espress.
poco cres
a tempo
mf espr.
408
f
mf espres
ev - 'ry blush that my love would hide, Is mir - ror'd for me in the tell - tale tide. And
f
mf espres
f
dim.

12
though you sleep on the far-thest isle, Round which these dimp-ling wa-ters smile. Yet
though you sleep, you sleep, the wa - ters smile. I've a
mf espress.
And though you sleep on the far - thest isle, the wa-ters
though you sleep, the wa - ters smile. A
mf espress.
416
I've a charm that can make the tide Bring you o-ver the wave to your lo - ver's
charm that can bring you o-ver the wave to your lo - ver's
smile. I've a charm that can bring you o-ver the wave to your lo - ver's
charm that can bring you o-ver the wave to your lo - ver's
dim.

420
poco rit.
rit.
side.
side.
side.
side.
poco rit.
rit.
p
424
a tempo
p
mm
But
p
mm
But
p
mm
But
mp espress.
p
Who, my friend, makes this ri - ver flow? The Spi - rit — he makes its rip - ples glow. But
a tempo
p espress.

poco rit.
a little slower
mp
I've a charm that can make the tide Bring you o - ver the wave to your
I've a charm that can make the tide, o - ver the wave to your
I've a charm that can make the tide, o - ver the wave to your
I've a charm that can make the tide, o - ver the wave to your
poco rit.
a little slower
rit.
pp
lo - ver's side.
lo - ver's side.
lo - ver's side.
lo - ver's side.
rit.
mp
pp

PART 4: ADULTHOOD

9. Summer Song

Inuit

* pronounced 'eye-ya'

52
beau - ti - ful, it is beau - ti - ful when the sum - mer comes at last.
56
f
A - ya! A - ya! A - ya! A - ya! A - ya! A - ya! A - ya! A - ya! A - ya -
T. & B. unis.
f
460
f
A - ya! A - ya! A - ya - ya.
S.
A.
-ya.
T.
B.

464
UPPER VOICES
A - ya! A - ya! A - ya! A - ya - ya.
sub. f
468
T. B.
T. & B. unis.
f
It is
f
472
UPPER VOICES
f
It is beau - ti - ful when the rein - deer come
T./B.
beau - ti - ful, it is beau - ti - ful when the rein-deer be-gin to come. It is
476
It is beau - ti - ful when the rein - deer
beau - ti - ful, it is beau - ti - ful when the rein-deer be-gin to come.

480
ER
ES
come.
Beau - ti - ful.
unis.
f
S.
A.
A - ya! A - ya! A - ya! A - ya!
A - ya! A - ya! A - ya! A - ya! A - ya-
T.
B.
f
484
f
When the roar - ing ri - ver rush-es from the hills in sum - mer.
-ya.
unis.
mf
A - ya! A -
unis.
(f)
When the ri - ver rush - es down.
mf

488
When the roar - ing ri - ver rush-es from the hills in sum - mer.
-ya!
A - ya! A -
When the ri - ver rush - es down.
492
A - ya! A - ya! A - ya! A - ya! A - ya!
unis.
A - ya! A - ya! A - ya!
-ya!
f
A - ya! A - ya! A - ya! A - ya! A - ya -
f
f

96
-ya.
-ya.
500 f
A - ya! A - ya! A - ya - ya. A - ya! A - ya! A - ya! A - ya -
f
A - ya!
f
sub. f

504
-ya.
A - ya! A - ya!
f

508
It is beau - ti -
SOPRANOS & ALTOS unis.
f
It is beau - ti - ful, it is beau - ti - ful when the
TENOR & BASSES unis.
f

12
-ful when the sum - mer,
sum - mer comes at last. It is beau - ti - ful, it is beau - ti - ful when the
516
sum - - mer comes at last. Beau - ti -
sum - mer comes at last. A - ya! A - ya! A - ya! A - ya!

520
- ful.
A - ya! A - ya! A - ya! A - ya!
A - ya! A - ya! A - ya! A - ya - ya - ya. A - ya! A - ya! A - ya! A - ya!
524
A - ya! A - ya! A - ya! A - ya - ya - ya - ya!
fff
A - ya! A - ya! A - ya! A - ya - ya - ya - ya!
fff
fff
ff
fff

PART 5: MIDDLE AGE

10. O Great Spirit

Dakota

543
ff
world. Hear me!
ff
f
ff
mf dim.
mp
549
pp
p
554
S.
p
I am small and weak, I need your power and wis-dom, Let me walk in beau-ty, let my
A.
p
I am small and weak, I need your power and wis-dom, Let me walk in beau-ty, let my

558
mp cresc.
eyes be glad be-hold - ing the red and gold-en dawn.
mp cresc.
eyes be glad be-hold - ing the red and gold-en dawn, red and gold-en dawn.
mp cresc.
be-hold - ing the red and gold-en, red and gold-en dawn, gold-en dawn.
mp cresc.
be-hold - ing the red and gold-en dawn, the red and
mp
562
Gold - en dawn.
p
Make my hands touch
p
gold-en dawn.
Make my hands touch
p

566
p cresc.
Make me wise that I may
p cresc.
Make me wise that I may
cresc.
all things you have made with love, Make me
all things you have made with love,
cresc.
570
cresc.
un - der-stand the sa - cred teach-ings you have taught.
cresc.
un - der-stand the sa - cred teach-ings you have taught.
cresc.
wise, make me wise, make me wise.
cresc.
cresc.
Make me wise, make me wise, make me wise.
cresc.

74
f
Help me, help me learn the les - sons hid - den in
f
f
577
ev - 'ry leaf and ev - 'ry stone. Help me,
poco rit.
a tempo
580
ff
help me. I seek strength, strength not to be
ff
poco rit.
a tempo
ff

583
great - er than my bro - ther but to con - quer the
586
e - ne-my with-in my - self.
mf espress.
dim.
590
BASSES p
B.
Make me rea - dy to come to you al-ways with a pure heart and with
p

94
p
mp
so when my life fades a - way,
so when my life fades a - way, life fades a - way,
so when my life fades, life fades a - way, fades a - way,
clear eyes, so when my life fades a - way, like the
dim.
598
like the set - ting sun, my spi - rit may
my spi - rit may
my spi - rit may
set - ting sun, my spi - rit may

602
come to you with ho - nour and with - out shame.
come to you with ho - nour and with - out shame.
come to you with ho - nour and with - out shame.
come to you with ho - nour and with - out shame.
pp sost.
607
poco cresc.
612
S.
A.
pp
O Great Spi - rit, whose
T.
B.
pp
pp

517
cresc.
voice speaks in the wind, whose breath gives life to all the world,
cresc.
cresc.
f
522
ff
mp
p
Hear me! Hear me! Hear
ff
mp
p
ff
mp
p
527
me!
pp sost.

PART 6: OLD AGE

11. In the house made of dawn

Navajo

* pronounced 'eye-ya'

† The piano reduction excludes the upper voices' parts for reasons of playability.

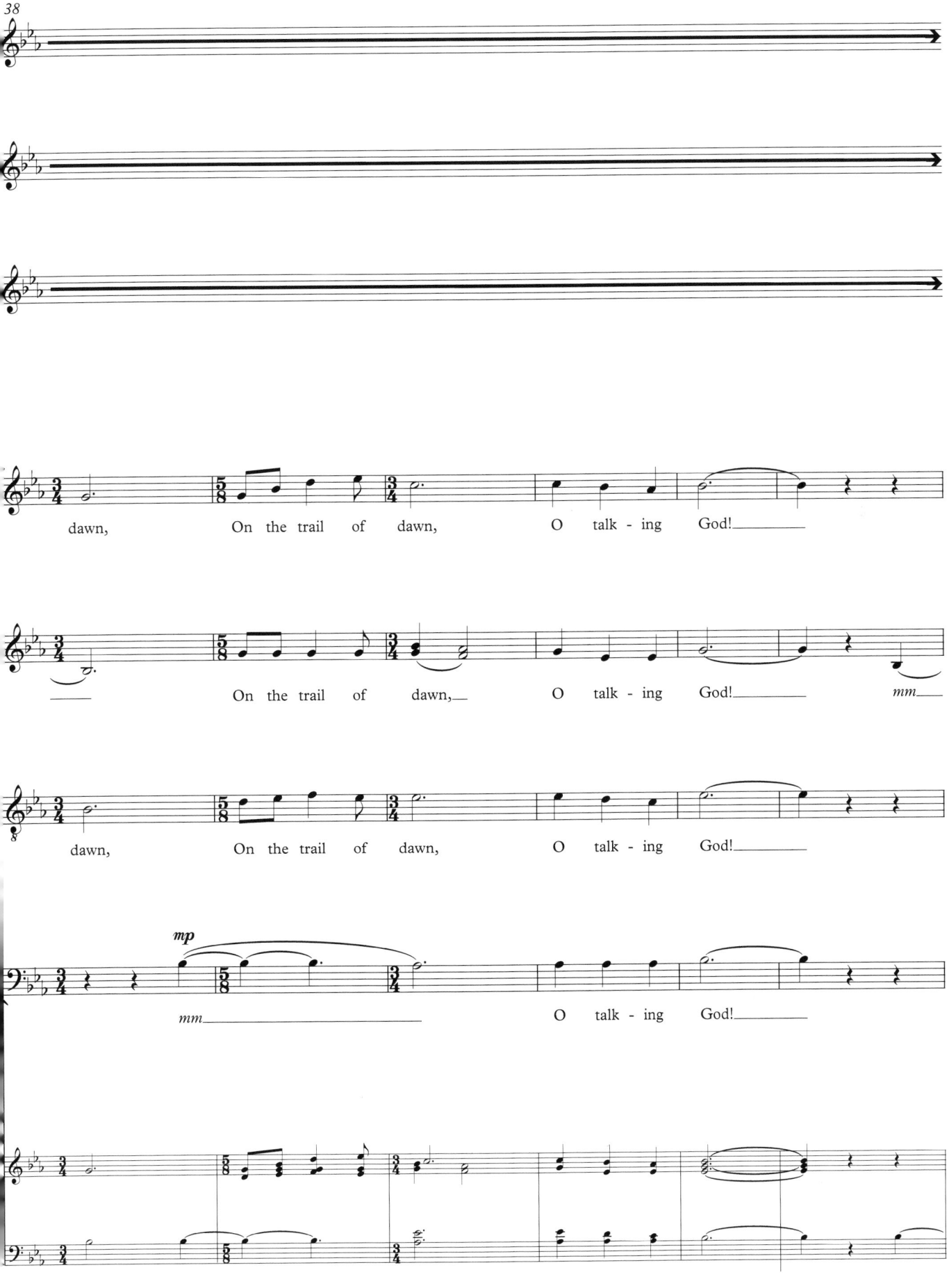
38
dawn, On the trail of dawn, O talk - ing God!
On the trail of dawn, O talk - ing God! mm
dawn, On the trail of dawn, O talk - ing God!
mp
mm O talk - ing God!

644
mp cresc.
A- ya, a - ya,
mp cresc.
A - ya, a - ya,
mp cresc.
A - ya, a - ya,
mf
Your feet, my feet re - store,
mf
Your feet, my feet re - store,
mf
Your feet, my feet re - store,
mf
Your feet, my feet re - store,
mf

51
mf
A - ya, a - ya,
A - ya, a - ya,
mf
mf
cresc.
f
Your limbs, my limbs re - store,
Your bo - dy, my bo - dy re - store,
Your
cresc.
f
Your limbs, my limbs re - store,
Your bo - dy, my bo - dy re - store,
Your
cresc.
f
Your limbs, my limbs re - store,
Your bo - dy, my bo - dy re - store,
Your
cresc.
f
Your limbs, my limbs re - store,
Your bo - dy, my bo - dy re - store,
Your
cresc.
f

656
f
dim.
A - ya, a - ya, A - ya, a - ya,
A - ya, a - ya, A - ya, a - ya,
A - ya, a - ya, A - ya, a - ya,
ff
mf
mind, my mind re - store, Your voice, my voice re - store,
mind, my mind re - store, Your voice, my voice re - store,
mind, my mind re - store, Your voice, my voice re - store,
mind, my mind re - store, Your voice, my voice re - store,

660
fade to nothing
fade to nothing
fade to nothing
p
plumes, my plumes re - store.
p
plumes, my plumes re - store.
p
plumes, my plumes re - store.
p
plumes, my plumes re - store.
p
plumes, my plumes re - store.
pp
With
p
plumes, my plumes re - store.
pp
With beau - ty be -
p
plumes, my plumes re - store.
pp
mm
Beau - ty,
p
pp

665
UPPER VOICES
S.
SOPRANOS unis.
pp
Beau - ty, beau - ty,
A.
ALTOS
pp
Beau - ty, beau -
S.1
pp
Beau - ty be - fore me, beau - ty,
S.2
pp
Beau - ty be - fore me, beau - ty, beau - ty,
A.1
pp
With beau - ty be - fore me,
A.2
pp
With beau - ty be - fore me, beau - ty,
T.
p
beau - ty be - fore you, Beau - ty be - fore me, With
B.1
p
- fore you, With beau - ty, with beau - ty be -
B.2
p
beau - ty, beau - ty,

70
poco cresc.
beau - ty, beau - ty, beau - ty, beau -
- ty,
poco cresc.
beau - ty, beau - ty, beau - ty,
p
Beau - ty be - hind me,
p
Beau - ty be - hind me,
mp cresc.
With
p
With beau - ty be - hind me,
beau - ty,
p
With beau - ty be - hind me, beau - ty,
mp cresc.
With beau - ty a -
mp cresc.
beau - ty be - hind you, beau - ty,
Beau - ty a - bove you,
mp cresc.
- hind you,
With beau - ty,
beau - ty a - bove you,
mp cresc.
beau - ty,
Beau - ty a - bove you, with
mp cresc.

675
- ty, beau - ty, beau - ty, beau - ty.
beau - ty, beau - ty, beau - ty.
mp cresc.
Beau - ty a - bove me, Beau - ty be - low me, Beau - ty be
beau - ty a - bove me, With beau - ty be - low you, with beau - ty,
mf
With beau - ty a - bove me, Beau - ty be - low me,
- bove me, beau - ty, beau - ty, Beau - ty be - low me, with
beau - ty a - bove you, Beau - ty be - low you, With beau - ty be -
beau - ty, beau - ty, beau - ty, beau - ty, Beau - ty be -
beau - ty a - bove you, Beau - ty be - low you, Beau - ty be -

80
p
Beau - ty, beau - ty, beau - ty.
p
Beau - ty, beau - ty, beau - ty.
- low me,
p
Beau - ty
p
Beau - ty a -
beau - ty,
p
With beau - ty a -
beau - ty,
p
With beau - ty a - round
- low, be - low me,
p
With beau - ty a - round you,
- low me,
p
Beau - ty a - round you, with
- low me,
p
with beau - ty, beau - ty,
p

685
UPPER VOICES
S.1
S.2
A.
p as opening
A - ya, a - ya,
p
A - ya, a - ya,
p
A - ya, a - ya,
S.1
a - round me, beau - ty.
S.2
- round me, beau - ty.
A.1
- round me, beau - ty.
p
mm
A.2
me, beau - ty.
p
mm
T.
beau - ty, beau - ty.
B.1
beau - ty, beau - ty.
B.2
beau - ty.
p

691
unis. mp
In the house of even-ing light, From the sto - ry made of even-ing light,
mm
mm
mp
In the house of even-ing light, From the sto - ry made of even-ing light,
unis. mp
mm
mp

695
On the trail of even - ing light,
On the trail of even - ing light,
each singer sings phrases independently and in own rhythm
p
On the trail of even - ing light,
It is fi- nish'd in beau -
each singer sings phrases independently and in own rhythm
p
On the trail of even - ing light,
It is fi - nish'd in beau - ty.
each singer sings phrases independently and in own rhythm
p
even - ing light,
It is

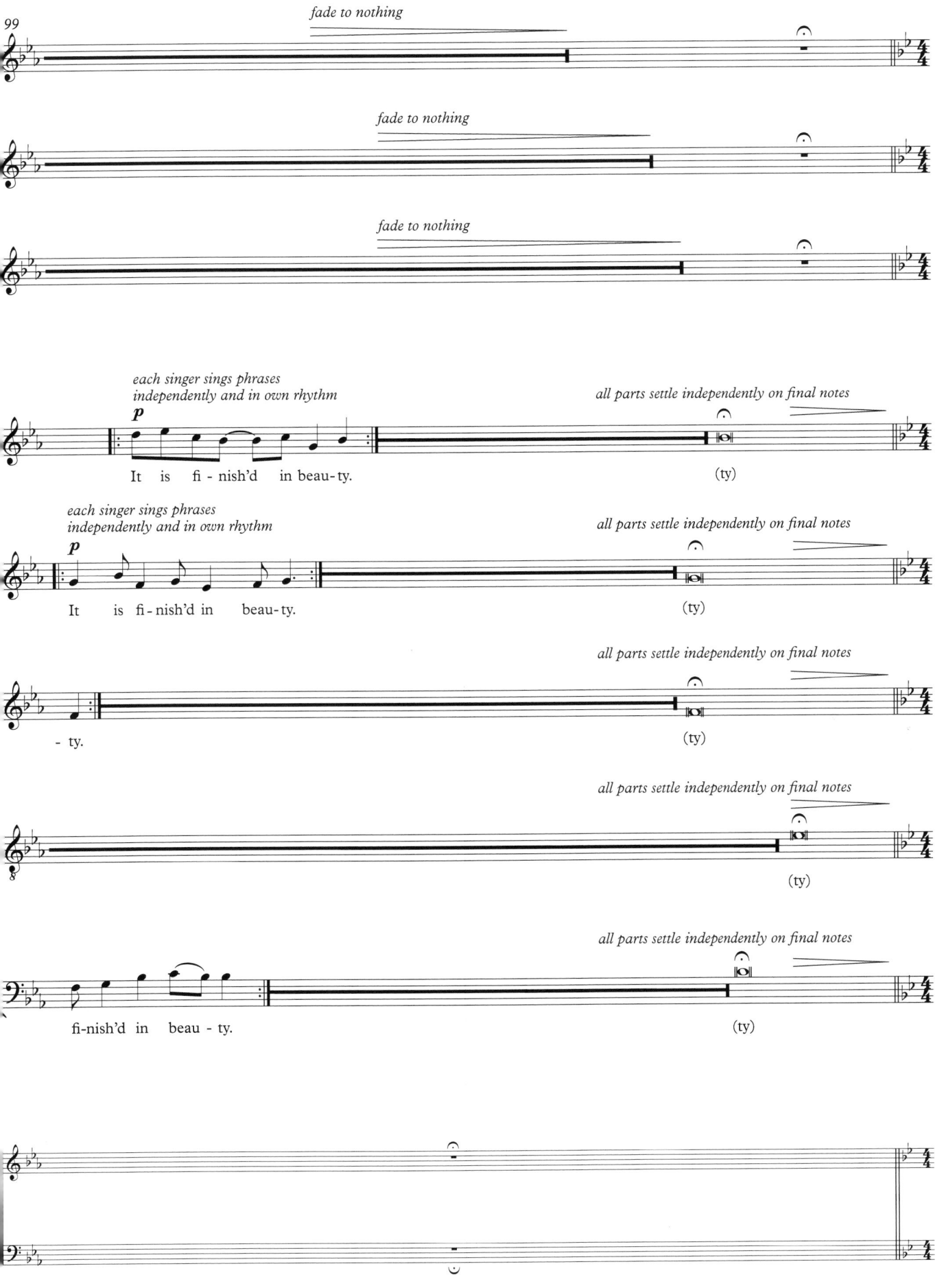
99
fade to nothing
fade to nothing
fade to nothing
each singer sings phrases independently and in own rhythm
p
It is fi - nish'd in beau- ty.
all parts settle independently on final notes
(ty)
each singer sings phrases independently and in own rhythm
p
It is fi - nish'd in beau- ty.
all parts settle independently on final notes
(ty)
- ty.
all parts settle independently on final notes
(ty)
all parts settle independently on final notes
(ty)
fi-nish'd in beau - ty.
all parts settle independently on final notes
(ty)

PART 7: DEATH

12. Farewell, my brother

Navajo

718
a tempo
mp
sounds.
And
pp
722
p dolce
when the har - vests ri - pen, and you hear voi - ces
Of all the beau - ti - ful
mp
p dolce
725
cresc.
mf
rit.
p
birds,
You will say, you will say,
'There is the
cresc.
mf
p
729
rit.
slower
trail of his soul.'
mp dolce
p

13. The sun's beams are running out / We wait in the darkness

Comanche / Iroquois

* Small notes are for rehearsal only.

38
The sun's, the sun's yel - low
p
The sun's beams are run - ning out,
sun's yel-low beams are run-ning out. The sun's beams are run - ning out,
sun's yel-low beams are run-ning out. The sun's beams are run - ning out,
sun's yel-low beams are run - ning out. The sun's beams are run - ning out,
sun's yel-low beams are run - ning out. The sun's beams are run - ning out,
beams are run - ning out, run - ning out, run-ning out.
A little quicker ♩ = c.66
742
run - ning out, run - ning out.
run - ning out, run - ning, run - ning out.
run - ning out, run - ning, run - ning out.
run - ning out, run - ning out.
run - ning out, run - ning, run - ning out.
A little quicker ♩ = c.66
p dolce

748
TENORS & BASSES unis.
mp
T./B.
We wait, we wait in the
751
dark - ness!
We wait, we wait
754
cresc.
in the dark - ness, dark - ness!
cresc.
757
mf espress.
Now no star is glow - ing;
Now no sun is
mf

760
T.
B.
f
shin - ing,
shin - ing,
763
unis.
p
shin - ing;
767
ER
CES
unis.
mp
We wait in the dark -
S.&A.
/A.
We wait, we wait in the dark - ness!
T.
We wait, we wait in the dark - - -
B.
We wait in the dark - - ness, the

770
- ness!
We wait
We wait, we wait in the
-ness!
We wait, we wait in the
dark - ness!
We wait in the
773
cresc.
in the dark - ness, dark - ness!
div.
mf
No
cresc.
dark - ness, dark - ness!
mf espress.
S.
A.
Now no star is
cresc.
dark - - - ness!
mf espress.
Now no star is
cresc.
dark - ness, the dark - ness!
mf espress.
Now no star is
cresc.
mf

776
ER
ES
star;
No
sun
is
S.
A.
glow - ing;
Now no sun is shin - ing,
T.
B.
779
f
shin - ing,
shin - ing;
f
shin - ing,
shin - ing;
ff
Come show us the
f
ff
f
ff

782
ff
Show us the way;
Our jour -
path - way;
Help in our jour - ney.

785
mf
mp
- ney.
No star,
mf
mp
Now no star is glow - ing;
Now no sun is
mf
mp
mf dim.
mp

88
unis.
p
mp
no
sun,
shin - -
shin - ing,
p
shin - ing,
shin - - - - ing,
p
p
791
- ing.
shin - ing.
shin - - - - ing.
shin - - - - ing, shin - - ing, shin - -
mp
shin - - - - ing.

794
Slow ♩ = c.56
pp
oo
p
ing.
We shall live a - gain,
p
p
Slow ♩ = c.56
p
799
oo
We shall live a - gain,

mm
mm
mm
p
live a - gain,
live
a - gain,
p
p
mm
mm
pp
a - gain,
a - gain.
pp
pp